All About

HURLING

Irene Barber

THE O'BRIEN PRESS
DUBLIN

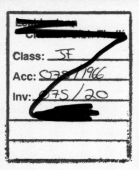
for Matt, Andrew and Martha

First published 2003 by The O'Brien Press Ltd,
20 Victoria Road, Dublin 6, Ireland.
Tel: +353 1 4923333; Fax: +353 1 4922777
E-mail: books@obrien.ie
Website: www.obrien.ie
Reprinted 2004

ISBN: 0-86278-808-0

British Library Cataloguing-in-publication Data
Barber, Irene
All About Hurling
1.Hurling (Game) - Juvenile literature
2.Camogie (Game) - Juvenile literature
I.Title
796.3'5
2   3   4   5   6   7   8   9   10
04   05   06   07   08   09   10

Acknowledgements
The author wishes to thank the following for their help and cooperation: Íde ní Laoghaire, Aoife
Dorney, John Raftery; Tom Fitzpatrick and Gerry Grogan; Brendan O'Connor of the *Tipperary
Star*; Liam O'Donoghue of Lár na Páirce Museum, Thurles; Eoin Kelly; DJ Carey; Brendan and
Gina Doley of Irish Timber and Forestry; Brian Gath; David Reale; Brendan Fullam; Séamus
King; PJ Cleary; Willie Dargan of O'Neills Sports; Mark Monahan; Anna Lynch; Pádraig Mac
Mathúna; Senan Murray; Catherine Rountree; Síle Wallace of Cumann Camógaíochta na nGael;
the staffs of the National Library of Ireland, Croke Park Museum, Sportsfile, Inpho,
the *Irish Examiner*.

Photograph credits
Sportsfile: front cover – main and bottom left, p8, p11 top, p12 bottom, p13 bottom, p14, p15, p18 top, p19
left, right and background, p22 top and bottom, p25, p29 middle right and bottom left, p30 bottom left, p31
top, middle, bottom left and right; Mark Monahan: title page – centre and background, p24 all, back cover;
Croke Park Museum: p10 bottom, p16 top left, p18 middle, p23 top and bottom, p30 top left; National Library
of Ireland: p4 top, p4-5 background, p5 top, p10 top three, p16 bottom; DACS: p4 middle; Lár na Páirce
Museum and Brendan O'Connor: p4 bottom, p28 middle left and right, p28 bottom left and right; Inpho: p16-17
centre and background, p29 top left and bottom right; John Knox: p22 left inset; *Irish Examiner*: p6 main, p20
top left and right, p21 top right and bottom left, p23 background picture, p30 bottom right, p31 centre right;
Lar Boland: p6 top left and right; Brendan Fullam (courtesy of): p18 bottom; Justin Nelson: p21 middle;
Michael Connor: drawings on pages 26 and 27; Pádraig Mac Mathúna (courtesy of): p28 top left; Séamus King
(courtesy of): p28 top right, photograph taken by F.J. Bigger, 1906; Anna Lynch: p32, family medals. Stories:
p6 *Our Games* 1965; p26 top, bottom Brendan Fullam; p8, p26 middle 'Carbery' (Paddy D. Mehigan).

Editing, typesetting: The O'Brien Press Ltd
Design and layout: The Design Office
Printing: Grafiche Industriali

IRENE BARBER   Teacher, former principal, past President of Children's Books Ireland. She comes from Fivealley,
Birr, the heart of the homeland of Offaly hurling. Her interest in hurling was fostered by her children, Andrew
and Martha, both of whom play with Faughs GAA club, Dublin, one of the oldest hurling clubs in the country.
Her husband, Matt Hume, coaches hurling to the boys at St Joseph's BNS, Terenure, Dublin.

COVER PHOTOS *Front*, main pic: Colm Ó Seanáin, Scoil Lorcáin, Monkstown, celebrates his team's third goal
against Gaelscoil Naomh Pádraig at Parnell Park – Cumann na mBunscol, Corann Ághais final, 2002;
inset: Kevin Broderick, Galway, chased by a Cork player. *Back* Maelruins vs Castleknock, 2003.

Contents

The History of Hurling

The first mention of hurling was in a story
about a match played over 3000 years ago.
A mythical tribe called the Firbolg ruled Ireland.
They played a hurling match against an invading tribe,
the Tuatha Dé Danann. The Firbolg won.

Playing hurling at Derrynane, Co. Kerry,
Daniel O'Connell's home, 1821

The most famous hurler of all was Setanta,
later called Cúchulainn – 'Hound of Culann'.
He killed a huge watchdog with one shot
from his hurley and ball.

In ancient times the laws in Ireland
were known as the Brehon Laws.
These laws mention compensation for anyone
injured or killed by a hurley or a *sliotar*.

The Normans invaded Ireland in the twelfth century.
The Normans were French, but they had settled
in England and Wales. They came to Ireland from there.
Their king in England tried to ban hurling
to stamp out Irish culture. But he didn't succeed.

'The Hurley Player', painted by Jack B Yeats

The oldest type of hurley

Daniel O'Connell

Hurling was very strong in Ireland
for many centuries. Gaelic chieftains
and, later, the new English landlords
supported the game. Often they had
their own teams of paid hurlers.

Boys play hurling in the
eighteenth century

At the end of the eighteenth century
there was a world-wide movement
of poor people looking for their rights.
In France the French Revolution happened.
In Ireland there was the 1798 rebellion.
This led to suspicion between landlords and tenants.
Landlords were no longer organising
hurling matches for their tenants.

There was a Great Famine in Ireland
in the middle of the nineteenth century.
The main food of the poor people at that time was potatoes.
Potatoes got a disease called blight and they rotted.
People were starving. It affected hurling,
as many people were sick, died or emigrated.
Also, fighting at matches was giving hurling a bad name,
and other sports were becoming popular –
by the late 1860s nearly every town in Ireland
had its own cricket club.

TALL
TALES

A hurling family of 1870 lived near the coast. One brother hit the ball up the wide chimney. His brother was outside and as the ball came down, he hit it back so accurately that it came down the chimney again.

Fionn MacCumhaill hurled the ball over the roof of his castle 21 times without letting it touch the ground. Each time he ran around the building to meet its fall.

The Hurley (camán)

Brian Gath from Offaly hand-making a hurley on a band-saw and testing it for strength and flexibility

TALL TALE but true

In 1925 there was a hurling match between an army team and Ballyheane club, Castlebar, County Mayo. At the start of the match a shovel lay at the back of one of the goals. During the match, the Ballyheane mid-fielder broke his hurley. As there were no spares, he walked off, thinking his game was over. His goalkeeper, Paddy Rainsford, shouted over to him: 'Hold on there, Mick, and take my hurley – I'll use the shovel.' This he did, stopping points and goals and displaying such wizardry with the shovel that the spectators were amazed. He kept the army at bay with the shovel for the rest of the match.

top of
the handle

The hurley is usually made from the wood of the ash tree.

About 1.2 metres of the butt of the tree is used,
right down where the trunk meets the roots.
This ensures that the grain of the wood
flows along the curve of the *bas* (boss).
This makes the hurley strong and flexible.

Ash trees that are about twenty years growing are used to
make hurleys. Ideally, the tree is cut down in the winter,
between November and February. At this time of year the sap
(the juice in the wood) is down. If there is sap in a hurley
it will warp (twist out of shape).

Once the ash is rooted out and sawn into lengths,
it is put in a drying shed for about nine months.
If there is too much moisture left in the hurley,
it will gradually lose weight as it dries out.
The hurler who bought it will not be happy
if the hurley is lighter each time he/she uses it.

middle of
the handle

Most hurleys nowadays are machine-made.
They are cut out of the wood using a hurley-shaped template.
They are machine-cut, a few at a time. Then they are trimmed
and sanded to give a smooth finish.

toe

A metal strip is put around the toe of the *bas* to prevent it
splitting. Players put tape on the handle of the hurley
to give a better grip.

bas (boss)

There is a shortage of home-grown ash.
At the moment about half the ash needed for hurleys
is imported from Europe. It is expected that
in about ten years, as new forests mature,
there will be enough home-grown ash to meet the demand.
Over 250,000 hurleys are made each year in Ireland.

band
(taped over
for camogie)

New designs are being investigated which use
man-made materials to make hurleys.

heel

The Sliotar

The hurling ball is called a sliotar (slith-her)

There are two different sizes of *sliotars*
used in hurling: sizes 4 and 5.
Size 4: 90g-110g, 21cm circumference.
Size 5: 100g-130g, 23-25cm circumference
Size 4 is used in camogie.
Size 5 is used in hurling.
The size of the *sliotar* has changed
from time to time.
Over a hundred years ago, the *sliotar*
was much bigger and heavier than it is now.
It was dark brown, three times the weight of the
modern ball: 303g, 33cm in circumference.
No wonder the scores were lower
and there was more ground hurling!

'Hurling (in the nineteen hundreds) was more tempestuous than it is today. The ball was heavier, the hurls were heavier and so were the men. I recall the great sweeping men from Tubberadora (Tipperary) and the neighbouring tillage parishes in the environment of Thurles town. They were sound ground hitters of great length and their forwards were a hurricane.' (Carbery)

In the 1950s the *sliotar* was smaller than a size 4 and it was very light. It was known as a Lalor ball.

There are a few different ways of making *sliotars*.
This is how one of the oldest suppliers, O'Neills,
make them:

The centre of the *sliotar* is made of **cork.**
Yarn (a mixture of cotton, polyester and
nylon threads) is wrapped around a small
ball of cork.

Then it is dipped in **latex,** a kind of liquid rubber.
When this dries out, the coat of latex gives
a hard, waterproof surface to the ball.

Two pieces of **leather** are then hand-sewn together
around the *sliotar.*

Yarn, coated with wax, is used to sew the pieces together.

The *sliotar* is polished and the cut ends of
the leather are blackened to give a
waterproof finish.

Some *sliotars*
are imported from
Asia but the highest
quality balls are
produced in Ireland.
Some say that imported
sliotars absorb a lot
of moisture and are
not as good.

The *sliotar* compared with the balls used in other sports:

rugby

American football jr.

soccer

cricket

baseball

hurling

tennis

golf

The Gaelic Athletic Association

Hurling and camogie are organised
in all thirty-two counties of Ireland
by the Gaelic Athletic Association (the GAA).

The GAA was set up at a meeting in
Miss Hayes's Commercial Hotel,
Thurles, County Tipperary, in 1884.
Its aims were to allow ordinary people
to compete in athletics and
to revive interest in hurling,
Gaelic football and handball.

Michael Cusack and Maurice Davin
helped set up the GAA.
Cusack was a teacher from Clare
who set up a school in Gardiner Place in Dublin.
Davin was a world-famous athlete from Tipperary.
He held the world hammer throwing record
and the Irish record in shot-put.
He became the first president of the GAA.

The GAA was a great success right from the beginning.
At first it was mainly involved in organising athletics events.
Later, the emphasis changed to
football, hurling and, to a lesser extent, handball.
The GAA agreed rules and organised competitions.
Clubs sprang up all over the country and,
as Cusack said, the association spread
'like a prairie fire'.

Nowadays the GAA is the biggest sporting
organisation in Ireland. And there are
GAA clubs all over the world.

Michael Cusack

Maurice Davin

[Established over a Century.]
THE COMMERCIAL AND FAMILY HOTE
AND POSTING ESTABLISHMENT,
THURLES.
LIZZIE J. HAYES, Proprietress.

An 1882 athletics event. This type of event was organised by the GAA in its early years.

The Trophies

The O'Duffy Cup

Since 1932, the All Ireland senior camogie champions have been presented with the O'Duffy Cup. This cup was presented by Mayo-man, Seán O'Duffy, when he set up the camogie championship in 1932. He was known as 'Mr Camogie' because he did so much to promote the game. It is said that every Sunday night he brought that day's camogie results down to Raidio Éireann in Henry Street in Dublin. This was to make sure that the results were broadcast. Seán O'Duffy was a freedom fighter and a trade union leader. The cup was designed and made by Margaret Meredith.

The MacCarthy Cup

The most sought after trophy in hurling is the Liam MacCarthy Cup. It was first presented for the 1921 senior hurling final between Dublin and Limerick. Limerick won.

Liam MacCarthy presented the cup to thank the GAA for all its work and to encourage greater interest in hurling. He was a wealthy Londoner but his parents were Irish. He had a great love for Ireland. The original cup was replaced with an almost exact replica in 1992. The new cup was made by James Mary Kelly from Kilkenny. It is stronger so that it can take the wear and tear. The old cup is on display in the GAA museum.

Winners of the All Ireland Camogie Championship 1932-2003

County	Wins
Dublin	26
Cork	20
Kilkenny	12
Antrim	6
Wexford	3
Tipperary	4
Galway	1

The All Ireland senior hurling final has been running every year since 1887, three years after the GAA was set up. Until 1921 it was the best club in each county, rather than a county team, that represented the county.

Winners of the All Ireland Senior Hurling Final 1887-2003

County	Wins
Cork	28
Kilkenny	28
Tipperary	25
Limerick	7
Wexford	6
Dublin	6
Offaly	4
Galway	4
Clare	3
Waterford	2
Kerry	1
Laois	1
London	1

Ulster

Hurling is stronger in other provinces than it is in Ulster.

Before the GAA was set up in 1884, there were two types of hurling played in Ireland.

Commons was played in the north, using a long narrow stick.

Iomáint was played in the south, using a shorter stick with a wider *bas*.

It is said that in order to choose between the two types of hurling, Michael Cusack organised a match. One team used a commons hurley, the other an *iomáint* hurley.

This game was played in the Phoenix Park on 18 January 1884.

The team with the short broad-based hurley won.

So *iomáint* became the type of hurling played by the GAA.

Maybe this goes some way to explaining why no Ulster county has ever won the All Ireland senior hurling final – they had a tradition of commons, not *iomáint*.

However, Antrim's camogie team more than make up for this. They have been All Ireland champions six times.

Donegal
Dún na nGall
Tír Chonaill
County song
'Mary from Dungloe'

Monaghan
Muineachán
The Farney County
County song
'The Town of Ballybay'

Down
An Dún
The Mourne County
County song
'The Star of the County Down'

Tyrone
Tír Eoghain
The Red Hand County
County song
'The Flower of Sweet Strabane'

Cavan
An Cabhán
The Breffni Blues
County song
'Come Back, Paddy Reilly'

Antrim
Aontroim
The Saffrons
County song
'The Green Glens of Antrim'

Fermanagh
Fear Manach
The Erne County
County song
'Leaving Enniskillen'

Armagh
Árd Mhacha
The Orchard County
County song
'The Boys from the County Armagh'

Derry
Doire
The Oak Leaf County
County song
'The Town I Loved So Well'

An Ulster player in action in 2000 – Alistair Elliot, Antrim.

Munster

Munster is the heartland of hurling.
This is where the GAA began
and this is still the strongest province.
From 1887 to 2003 a team from Munster
won the All Ireland senior hurling final
in sixty-six of those 116 years.
From 1932 to 2003 a Munster team
won the All Ireland senior camogie final
in twenty-four of those seventy-one years.
Cork is the most successful
hurling county in Munster,
winning the hurling title twenty-eight times.
Cork were camogie champions twenty times,
second only to Dublin.
Tipperary were hurling champions
on twenty-five occasions and
camogie champions on four occasions.
All counties in Munster were
All Ireland hurling champions at least once.
No other province can match this.

Clare
An Clár
The Banner County

County song
'My Lovely Rose of Clare'

Tipperary
Tiobraid Árann
The Premier County

County song
'Slievenamon'

Waterford
Port Láirge
The Deise County

County song
'Dungarvan, My Home Town'

Cork
Corcaigh
The Rebels

County song
'The Banks of My Own Lovely Lee'

Kerry
Ciarraí
The Kingdom

County song
'Rose of Tralee'

Limerick
Luimneach
The Shannonsiders

County song
'Limerick, You're a Lady'

Joe Deane, Cork,
and Brian Greene, Waterford,
in the Munster Final, 2003.

Leinster

Kilkenny is by far the most successful
hurling county in Leinster.
The Cats have won the
All Ireland senior hurling final
on twenty-eight occasions between 1887 and 2003.
That's the same as Cork,
the most successful Munster county.
Dublin hold the record for winning the most
All Ireland senior camogie championship titles,
having won twenty-six times
over the seventy-one years of the competition.
Kilkenny have been
All Ireland camogie champions twelve times,
and Wexford three times.
Wexford and Dublin were hurling champions six times,
Offaly four times and Laois once.

Offaly, the
'Comeback Kids'

Longford
An Longfort
No nickname!

County song
'Abbeyshrule'

Laois
Laois
The Moore County

County song
'Lovely Laois'

Carlow
Ceatharlach
The Floral County

County song
'Follow Me Up to Carlow'

Dublin
Baile Átha Cliath
The Dubs

County song
'Molly Malone'

Westmeath
An Iarmhí
The Lake County

County song
'Westmeath Bachelor'

Kilkenny
Cill Chainnigh
The Cats

County song
'The Rose of Mooncoin'

Wicklow
Cill Mhantáin
The Garden County

County song
'The Meeting of the
Waters'

Meath
An Mhí
The Royals

County song
'Beautiful Meath'

Offaly
Uíbh Fháilí
The Faithful County

County song
'The Offaly Rover'

Wexford
Loch Garman
The Model County

County song
'Boulavogue'

Kildare
Cill Dara
The Lily Whites

County song
'The Curragh of Kildare'

Louth
An Lú
The Wee County

County song
'The Turfman from Ardee'

Connaught

Mayo
Maigh Eo
The Yew County
County song
'Moonlight in Mayo'

Galway
Gaillimh
The Tribesmen
County song
'The Fields of Athenry'

Galway is the strongest hurling
and camogie county in Connaught.
Galway brought the MacCarthy Cup
west of the Shannon four times,
first in 1923 and then, after a long wait,
three times in the 1980s.
The O'Duffy cup crossed the Shannon in 1996.

Galway (Meelick Club) took part in
the first ever All Ireland final.
This championship began in 1887
but the final wasn't played until
1 April 1888, in Birr.

Roscommon
Ros Comáin
The Rossies
County song
'The Men of Roscommon'

Leitrim
Liatroim
The Wild Rose County
County song
'Lovely Leitrim'

Sligo
Sligeach
The Yeats County
County song
'The Salley Gardens'

Kevin Broderick
from Galway being
chased by Cork players.

15

Croke Park

All the big games are played on the GAA's finest pitch, Croke Park.
Since its recent face-lift, Croke Park is now a world class stadium.
It has seats for 79,000 people, a state-of-the-art pitch, a museum, ninety-seven meeting rooms, bars and restaurants.
Croke Park is on the north side of Dublin city, just outside the city centre.
It is situated between the Royal Canal and a railway line.
The stadium is surrounded by houses on all sides.
Croke Park is named after Dr Thomas Croke, Roman Catholic Archbishop of Cashel (above).
He was the GAA's first patron.
The GAA bought the Croke Park grounds for £3500 pounds (€4444) in 1913.

The recent redevelopment cost €200 million.
The size of the Croke Park pitch is 142m by 86m.
This is bigger than a soccer pitch.
In some Italian stadia, the seating is at a 45-degree angle to the ground.
In Croke Park the angle is not more than 30 degrees.
This prevents the vertigo effect.
There are huge crowds in Croke Park and strong county rivalry on All Ireland final day.
But there is seldom any hooliganism.
Fans of opposing counties sit or stand beside each other and usually the banter is good-humoured.

NALLY STAND

HILL 16

HOGAN STAND

AMRITZAR REPEATED IN DUBLIN

Armed Forces of the Crown Kill Player and Spectators in Croke Park

AGONISING SCENES ON FOOTBALL FIELD

Eleven or Twelve Persons, including a Woman, Killed, and from Eighty to One Hundred Wounded

NALLY STAND

This stand was named after Pat Nally, a Mayo athlete and nationalist, and a strong supporter of Michael Cusack. He died in Mountjoy jail in 1891 after a ten-year sentence. He had been in prison for treason. A new terraced area, which will have standing room for 16,000, will replace this stand.

CUSACK STAND

HILL 16

This was the first terrace to be built. It was made from the rubble of the buildings in Sackville Street (now O'Connell St). These buildings were destroyed in the 1916 Rising when the Irish rose up against the British.

CUSACK STAND

This is named after Michael Cusack, a Clare schoolteacher. He was one of the founders of the GAA.

CANAL END

THE CANAL END STAND

This refers to the Royal Canal which forms a boundary on the city end of Croke Park. The canal was completed in 1789 and was used to transport goods, like Guinness and coal. When railways were built in the middle of the next century, trains were used instead.

HOGAN STAND

This stand was built in 1924 and named after Michael Hogan. He was the Tipperary captain who was shot during a football match at Croke Park in 1920. British forces opened fire on players and spectators. Here is an extract from a newspaper report in the next day's *Freeman's Journal*:

'The bullets came as thick as hail, dealing out death in their swift passage; a wild scene of panic ensued, and women and children were knocked down and walked on.'

Thirteen people were killed. Almost one hundred were wounded. The attack was in revenge for the shooting, earlier that day, of alleged British spies by the Irish. Fourteen members of the British Secret Service were killed and five wounded. This event is now known as 'Bloody Sunday'.

17

Camogie

Camogie is a game, very like hurling, which is played by girls and women.

The name comes from the Irish word *camóg* which means a stick with a crook at the end of it. The Camogie Association was set up in 1904 and it is one of the largest female sporting organisations in Ireland.

In the early days, the players played in ground-length skirts and it was a foul to stop the *sliotar* with your skirt (on purpose)!

Una O'Donoghue does a solo run for Cork, 2002.

Camogie Greats

Kathleen Mills (1923-1996) of Dublin has fifteen All Ireland medals, that's more than any other GAA player, even Christy Ring.

Angela Downey was born into a Kilkenny hurling family. She played for her county for twenty-five years, 1972 to 1995. In that time she played in fourteen All Ireland finals and she won a total of twelve All Ireland medals. Angela remembers the magic of Croke Park in 1991: *'Meeting the President [Mary Robinson] was a huge thrill. I had led my team behind the Artane Boys' Band and walked up the steps to collect the cup. We felt we were being treated like the hurlers.'*

Una O'Connor (Dublin) has thirteen All Ireland medals.

Playing camogie in 1904, complete with long skirts! Note the old-style hurleys. Cuchulainn's camogie club.

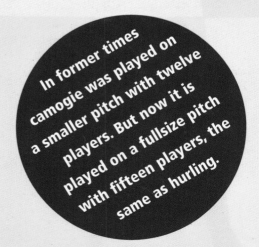

Accepting a wedge of orange, half-time standard fare. Kathleen Mills is seated on the left.

In former times camogie was played on a smaller pitch with twelve players. But now it is played on a fullsize pitch with fifteen players, the same as hurling.

18

Sinéad Millea, Kilkenny, takes a powerful swing, 2001.

There are very few differences between camogie and hurling.
The following are the main differences:

	Camogie	Hurling
Playing gear	The whole team, including the goal-keeper, must wear the same jersey. All wear skirts or divided skirts.	The goalkeeper must wear a different jersey. The players wear shorts.
Sliotar	Weight: 90-110g Size: 21cm in circumference	Weight: 110-120g Size: 23-25cm in circumference
Scores	A handpassed goal is allowed. A 45-metre free is awarded.	A handpassed goal is not allowed. A 65-metre free is awarded.
Dropping of hurley	A hurley may be dropped to handpass the *sliotar*.	This is a foul in hurling.
Yellow and red cards	Red card only is used to send a player off for dangerous play.	Yellow card may be used for first offence. Red card is used to send a player off.
Hurley	The band on the *bas* of the hurley is taped over.	The band is not taped over.

Mick Mackey

1912-1982

Mick Mackey played for Limerick.
He was the first Superstar,
the first Playboy of Hurling.
He loved the glory and drama
and challenge of the game
and it is said that he played
with a smile on his face.
He is famous for his solo run.

Mick Mackey wore shorts that were made
from the recycled cloth of old flour bags.
The empty flour bags were washed,
the paper labels scraped off them,
the seams ripped and then the cloth
was bleached to make it white.
A local dressmaker cut out and sewed up a pair of shorts.
These were for special occasions!

Mackey could be a bit of a trickster.
Once he injured his right knee
while on tour in America.
On his return, in order to fool the opposition,
he put a large bandage on his left, uninjured knee.
It must have worked because
he scored 5-3 from a total of 8-5 to Tipperary's 4-6.

He was interested in all sports
and attended rugby and soccer games.
At this time the GAA banned all its players
from playing or attending those 'foreign' games.
What could they do about Mick?
If they banned such a famous player
there would be uproar.
So they made him a member of
the Vigilance Committee – a spy!
His job was to see if any GAA players
were attending these games
and to report back if they were.
Now he could officially attend the matches!

Mackey has a word with the opposition, 1939.

Mackey's well-worn hurley

Mick Mackey won:
3 All Ireland medals
8 Railway Cup medals
5 Munster Championship medals
5 National Hurling League medals

Christy Ring

1920-1979

Christy Ring is regarded as
the greatest hurler of all time – a modern Cúchulainn.
He played for Cork in the 1940s and 1950s.
He was brilliant: strong, fast, intensely focused,
intelligent and skilful. He once wrote: 'Hurling has always
been a way of life with me. It was never my ambition
to play the game for the sake of winning All Ireland medals
or breaking records, but to perfect the art
as well as possible.'

Christy Ring won:
8 All Ireland medals
18 Railway Cup medals
9 Munster championships medals
4 National Hurling League medals

Here is what others had to say about Christy Ring:

*'He grew up to be a man who moved like a dancer, was as strong
as a bull, quick as a top class sprinter and wielded a camán like
a sorcerer.'* **Eamonn Sweeney**, writer and journalist

'Hurling was his whole life.'
Ring's brother, **Willie John**

'He could make a ball talk.'
Jimmy Doyle, Tipperary hurling legend

*'He had a wider range of skills than any
other player that I ever saw'*
Con Murphy, Cork hurler

'That scar there on my jaw is from Christy Ring.'
John Doyle, Tipperary hurler

*'He was a grand singer. Himself and Jim Barry
would sing on the way home. He was
great company and he was very witty.
He was a brilliant, very intelligent man,
but then a shy man as well.'*
Willie John Daly, Cork hurler

Mackey (umpire) and Ring in 1957.
Mackey had raised the green flag to
signal a goal for Tipperary, but the
referee over-ruled it. Here, the two
famous men exchange a few words.
Nobody knows what they said but plenty
of people have been guessing since then!

Christy Ring died suddenly at the age of 58.

Ned Power flies through the air
to get away from Christy Ring's swinging
hurley, 1959 Munster Final.

DJ Carey

DJ Carey is the best-known hurler
living in Ireland at this time.
He is known as 'The Dodger'
and comes from Gowran, County Kilkenny.
Eddie Keher, himself a hurling legend in Kilkenny,
describes DJ as 'the most complete hurler I have ever seen'.

DJ was born in 1970 and from four years of age
he looked like he would be a good hurler.
He played for his primary school, Gowran National School;
his club, Young Ireland; his secondary school,
St Kieran's College and his county, Kilkenny.

By 2002, DJ Carey had won:
4 All-Ireland senior hurling medals
3 Railway Cup medals
7 Leinster Championship medals
2 National Hurling League medals.
He has nine All-Star Awards.
He was named All-Star Hurler of the Year 2000,
and GPA Player of the Year 2000.

DJ Carey was one of the founder members
of the Gaelic Players Association (GPA).
This association was set up in 1999
to look after the interests of players.
DJ Carey had this to say:
'I'm a GAA player and for me there's
no better organisation in the world.
And as far as I'm concerned
the players should have their say
and hopefully they'll have a stronger say in the future.'

DJ Carey has this advice for young players:
'Spend ten to fifteen minutes every day developing your hurling skills.
This will give you a huge advantage.'

Famous Commentators

The two best known voices in radio broadcasting of GAA matches are Micheál O'Hehir (left with Tipperary hurling legend, John Doyle) and Micheál Ó Muircheartaigh (below).

Micheál O'Hehir began radio broadcasting in 1938. For many older people when they think of childhood Sunday afternoons, they immediately think of Micheál O'Hehir's voice on the radio. Before the matches were televised, he could paint pictures in people's minds. To listen to him was nearly as good as being there. His love of the game shone through and his exciting commentaries were greatly appreciated all over the world. In the early days he often had to work under difficult conditions. In 1950 in Nowlan Park, Kilkenny, Micheál was broadcasting from a car placed on top of a lorry! He sat cross-legged on the roof and gave his commentary. As time went by, the roof of the car began to cave in under his weight. A friend had to keep the roof from collapsing while Micheál finished his match commentary.

Micheál Ó Muircheartaigh began broadcasting in 1949. His distinctive voice and colourful commentaries have made him a household name. Here are some examples of his style:

'Pat Fox has it on his hurl and is motoring well now … but here comes Joe Rabitte hot on his tail … I've seen it all now, a Rabitte chasing a Fox around Croke Park!'

'He grabs the sliotar, he's on the 50 … he's on the 40 … he's on the 30 … he's on the ground.'

'Stephen Byrne with the puck out for Offaly … Stephen, one of twelve … all but one are here to-day, the one that's missing is Mary, she's at home minding the house … and the ball is dropping i lár na páirce …'

'Seán Óg Ó Hailpín … his father's from Fermanagh, his mother's from Fiji – neither a hurling stronghold.'

Tom's Top Tips

1 Pick a hurley that is the right length for your height.

2 Place the hand you use when writing at the top of the handle.

3 Leave the other hand free to move up and down the handle.

4 Buy your own tennis-type ball and balance the ball on your hurley as you walk and run.

5 Using your hurley and ball, play against a tall wall.

6 Keep your eye on the ball at all times when playing.

7 Ask a friend to get a hurley and enjoy striking the ball to each other.

8 With your friend invite others at school to play hurling on the local green space.

9 Why don't all of you join the local GAA club where you will get more advice from the hurling coach?

10 Shake hands with your hurley every day.

Tom Fitzpatrick is the Secretary of Cumann na mBunscol, Áth Cliath, which organises hurling, camogie, football and athletics in primary schools. Tom is also GAA Officer in Dublin Colleges of Education for trainee teachers.

An Poc fada

(the 'long hit')

The Poc Fada is a hurling skills competition.
It takes place each year in the Cooley Mountains in County Louth.
The winner is the one who hits his sliotar
with the hurley in the least amount of hits
around a 5km course.
The course is cross-country, in rough, hilly land.
A team of score-keepers walks with each competitor
to lead the way, to mark where the sliotar falls
and to keep the score.
The winner receives the Corn Cuailgne trophy.

The record is 50 hits.
That makes an average of 100 metres for each hit.
100 metres is almost two-thirds the length
of a full-size hurling pitch.

The Poc Fada suits goalkeepers
as they can usually hit the ball way
down the field.
They frequently win this event.

The Poc Fada competition
began in 1961.
The idea comes from
the ancient stories.
It is based on a journey Setanta
(the young Cúchulainn)
took from Dundalk to Armagh.
It is said that he hit his sliotar
all the way
hitting it very far ahead,
then running to catch up with it
before it fell.

Colin Byrne of Wicklow, August 2000

'As Dundalk's Gerry Dunne paused to wipe the sweat off his brow a loud "crack" split the the air and dozens of heads turned to watch a hurtling ball arc into the sky above the rocky mountainside before landing in a bed of purple heather. "This is as primitive as it gets. It's man against nature," said the smiling Dunne, a scorekeeper at the Poc Fada championship on Ireland's rugged Cooley mountains.'

The Boston Herald

'The Poc Fada is a truly unique event within the GAA and its roots can be traced back to the great Cúchulainn himself,'
Sean Kelly, President of the GAA.

Hurling Stories

'I was playing an under-16 match and a flock of sheep came out on the field in the middle of the game. The match was stopped so they could hunt the sheep off!' Sharon McMahon (Clare), Féile na nGael skills winner 2001.

The Thunder and Lightning Final

World War II had just broken out. Hitler was heading for Poland as supporters were making their way to Croke Park for the 1939 All Ireland hurling final between Kilkenny and Cork. The teams were well matched but at half time Kilkenny were in the lead. During the second half the rain came down in torrents. Lightning flashed and thunder rumbled. But still they battled on, regardless of storm or war. The play was fast and furious and the sides were level with minutes to go. Owen McCann takes up the story: 'Suddenly from nowhere Jimmy Kelly, a dashing Noreside [Kilkenny] midfielder, powered in to pick up the clearance and score a glorious point to give his side their fourth Liam MacCarthy Cup win of the decade.' The rain was still lashing down, causing the dye from their shirts to run into their shorts, but nobody noticed, well, nobody from Kilkenny.

A Man and His Hurl (Carbery)

'I had a few hurls broken before I got one to suit me – a hurl I can never forget. A delightful hurley of willow ash that would bend round your waist and spring back like a steel blade of Toledo. At first it was carefully laid beneath the mattress to keep the line true. There was little necessity – it was well seasoned. It stood me well for four seasons and I cried bitter tears the day I broke it beyond repair.'

A Long Journey (Brendan Fullam)

'The story is told that in one of these All Ireland hurling successes (in the 1890s) the men of Tubberadora walked to Thurles, got the train to Dublin, played and won the final, got the train back to Thurles, walked to Tubberadora – and milked the cows.'

Ground hurling

The perfectly-shaped goalie

A breaking ball

The Changing Rules

Soon after the GAA was set up in 1884,
a formal set of rules was drawn up.
In the early days, there could be
up to 21 players on a team.
In 1892 this was reduced to 17
and in 1913 teams were reduced again to 15,
as they are today.
In the early days, the team with
the greatest number of goals was the winner.
If no goals were scored, the team
with the greatest number of points
won the match.
From 1892 to 1896 goals were worth five points.
Then they were re-valued at three points,
as they are today.
Wrestling was allowed in hurling matches
up to the end of 1886.

In the early days, the game was started by the referee throwing in the ball between two lines of opposing players. Now the game is started by the referee throwing in the ball between the four mid-fielders.

A bit of a shamozzle

A square ball

The Kings vs the Wee County

The Cats vs the Tribesmen

Guess who?

Then

The Clare team of 1914, All Ireland hurling champions. Their trainer was Jim O'Hehir, father of the commentator Micheál. Clare supporters had a long wait for their second All Ireland win.

A young hurler, c.1906.

Helmets were not worn until recent years. This cap was presented to Johnny Leahy, Tubberadora, Co. Tipperary, for his victory in the 1916 All Ireland final.

This is where the first All Ireland final was played in 1888. It is in Birr, County Offaly. Compare this field to Croke Park, opposite.

Now

Clare's second All Ireland winning team – 1995.

Up for the Match

Artane Boys' Band – the oldest boy band?
Since 1886, every year the Artane Boys' Band
have played at GAA finals in Croke Park.
The band used to be selected from boys in the
Artane Industrial School, set up by the Christian Brothers
in 1872. Artane was a home for boys as young as seven
who had been in trouble or who were orphans
or whose families could not look after them.
The band built up a great reputation.
Their music and their scarlet and blue uniforms
were part of the scene at the big matches in Croke Park.
In the 1990s it emerged that life for some of the boys in Artane
was very lonely and often cruel.

The school closed down in 1969 and in the same year
a fire destroyed their instruments, uniforms and music.
But they began again and now band boys are enrolled from schools
around Dublin's northside. They meet in the Artane School of Music
and continue to entertain at Croke Park. Past members of the band have formed
a senior band, and they march, in navy uniforms, behind the boys in Croke Park.
Larry Mullen, of U2, played with the Artane Boys' Band for a short time.

At a camogie All Ireland final against Cork, Kilkenny player Angela Downey lost both her hurley – and her skirt! Despite this she palmed the sliotar into the net and scored a goal!

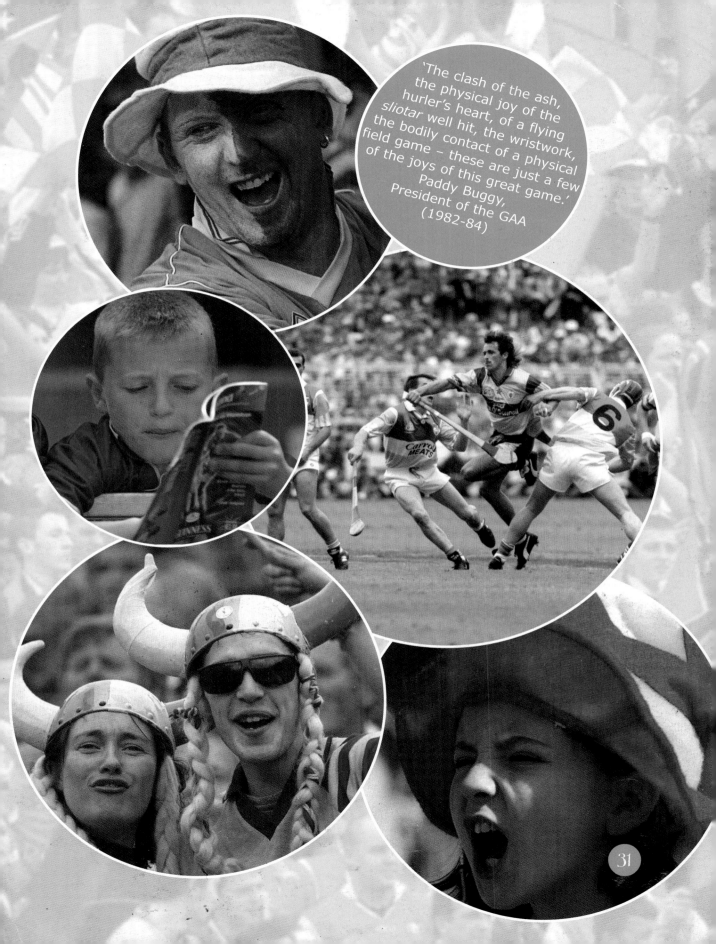

'The clash of the ash, the physical joy of the hurler's heart, of a flying *sliotar* well hit, the wristwork, the bodily contact of a physical field game – these are just a few of the joys of this great game.'
Paddy Buggy,
President of the GAA
(1982-84)

31

Bibliography & Index

Brehony, Martin, and Keenan, Donal, *The Ultimate Encyclopedia of Gaelic Football & Hurling* (Carlton Books, 2001) 1-84222-336-4

De Burca, Marcus, *The GAA, A History* (Gill & Macmillan, 2000) 0-71713-109-2

Fullam, Brendan, *Giants of the Ash* (Wolfhound Press, 1991) 0-86327-315-7

Fullam, Brendan, *The Final Whistle* (Wolfhound Press, 2000) 0-86327-826-4

Fullam, Brendan, *Captains of the Ash* (Wolfhound Press, 2002) 0-86327-900-7

Hayes, Seamus, *Come on the Banner!* (Gill & Macmillan) 0-71712-442-8

Humphries, Tom, *Green Fields* (Weidenfeld & Nicolson, 1996) 0-29783-566-1

Keane, Colm, *Hurling's Top 20* (Mainstream Publishing, 2002) 1-84018-577-5

King, Seamus J., *A History of Hurling* (Gill & Macmillan, 1998) 0-71712-712-5

Sweeney, Eamonn, *Munster Hurling Legends* (The O'Brien Press, 2002) 0-86278-773-4

Fleming, Diarmaid, 'Design Is Right on the Ball', *Construction News*, 9 November 2000

Websites

www.cul4kidz.com (the official GAA site for young people)
www.gaa.ie (this site has a link to Cumann na mBunscol))

Museums

GAA Museum, Croke Park, Dublin 3. Phone (01) 8558176
Lár na Páirce Museum, Slievenamon Road, Thurles, Co. Tipperary. Phone (0504) 23579
Lory Meagher Heritage Centre and Museum, Tullaroan, Co. Kilkenny. http://kilkenny.gaa.ie

County Songs *All Ireland Songs and Heroes, A Musical Tribute to 32 Counties*, Dolphin Records

Index (bold type denotes picture)

Medals: (above) Kilflynn (Co. Kerry) School Champions, 1928; (right) Junior Hurling Championship, Mayo, 1935, Winners: Ballyheane (*reverse*)

Invaders and Settlers

Nicola Baxter

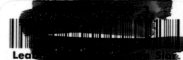

W
FRANKLIN WATTS
NEW YORK • LONDON • SYDNEY

First published in 1994 as
Craft Topics: Invaders and Settlers

This edition first published in 1997

© Franklin Watts 1994, 1997

The Watts Publishing Group
96 Leonard Street
London EC2A 4RH

Franklin Watts
14 Mars Road
Lane Cove
NSW 2066

ISBN: 0 7496 2822 7

Editor: Hazel Poole
Designer: Sally Boothroyd
Photography by: Peter Millard
Illustrator: Ed Dovey
Additional picture research by: Juliet Duff
Cover design: Kirstie Billingham
National Curriculum guidelines: Nicola Baxter
Puzzlers' Page: Anita Ganeri

A CIP catalogue record for this book is available from the British Library.

Printed in Great Britain

CONTENTS

THE FAR EDGE OF EUROPE

From the earliest times, people have travelled from their homes to find better lives for themselves and their families. The new skills, ideas and languages that they bring to the country where they settle may change for ever the lives of the people already living there and the history of the country itself.

At the time when Celtic peoples were moving westward into Britain, the great civilisations of Greece and Rome grew up around the Mediterranean. From small beginnings in Rome, the Roman Empire spread in all directions. In the first century AD, Britain became the most northerly part of the Roman Empire.

A THOUSAND YEARS OF INVASIONS

It is almost a thousand years since Britain was last invaded and conquered by an army from overseas. This was when the Normans, under the leadership of Duke William of Normandy, invaded in 1066. But for a thousand years before that, many different peoples came to settle in the British Isles. They knew that Britain had rich supplies of wood, metal and farmed produce. The changes that these invaders brought to Britain are still part of our lives today.

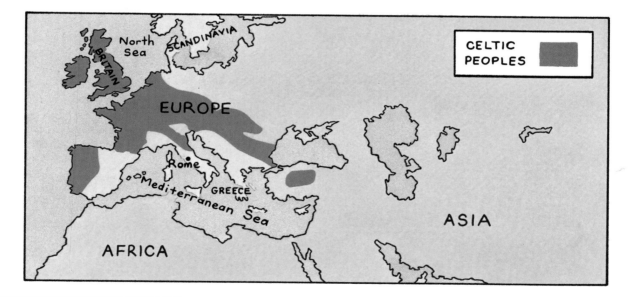

3500 BC onwards people from western Europe settle in Britain.

55 BC The Roman Julius Caesar arrives in Britain.

AD 43 The Romans invade southern Britain.

AD 406 The Romans leave Britain. The Anglo-Saxons begin to invade northern and eastern Britain.

THE ANCIENT BRITONS

The people who lived in Britain 2,000 years ago are known as Britons, but they too had come from more eastern parts of Europe. They were of Celtic origin, the ancestors of many of the people who live in Wales today. The roots of their Celtic languages can still be traced in modern Welsh and Gaelic languages.

The time in which the ancient Britons lived is known as the Iron Age because they made and used iron tools. In fact, the Celts were very skilled at working many kinds of metal.

Most Celts lived by farming. Large family groups farmed the land and raised animals for food and clothing. Traces of their fields can sometimes be seen today, but more obvious are the huge mounds of earth that they built to protect themselves from attack.

▲ *Many Iron Age earthworks can still be seen. This fort at Maiden Castle in Dorset was protected by four great earth walls.*

We cannot read what the Celtic Britons themselves felt and thought because until the Roman invasion they did not read or write. Their knowledge of what had happened came from spoken stories or songs. This is called oral history.

The Celts in Britain were not isolated from the rest of Europe. Traders brought goods from other parts of the Roman Empire long before the Roman invasion.

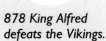
793 The Vikings begin to raid Britain.

878 King Alfred defeats the Vikings.

1066 The Normans invade Britain.

THE ROMAN INVASION

By the time the Romans invaded Britain in AD 43, they already had a vast empire. They were used to taking over new lands and people and had very efficient armies and army commanders who knew how to take control quickly and completely.

At the time of the invasion, the Romans had already had contact with parts of Britain for nearly a hundred years. In 55 BC Julius Caesar, who had been fighting in what is now France, crossed the Channel and subdued a few tribes. His visit may have been meant only as a warning to the Britons not to help the French tribes fight the Romans.

About 40,000 Roman soldiers took part in the invasion of AD 43. They had better weapons than the British troops and they were more carefully trained and organised. Some tribes fought hard against the invaders, but others were happy to welcome new opportunities to trade with the whole Roman Empire.

As soon as the south-east was secure, the Emperor Claudius himself came to accept the surrender of the local leaders of the British tribes at what is now Colchester in Essex.

This bronze shield shows the skill of Celtic craftsmen before the Roman invasion. They used beautifully flowing designs to decorate their metalwork. The shield was found in the River Thames. ▶

▲ *Before they could get close to the Romans, the British soldiers were attacked by a hail of javelins. In close fighting, their longer swords were difficult to use and, unlike the Romans, they had very little armour.*

6

MAKE A CELTIC SHIELD

Ask a grown-up to help you with this, as the knife blade will be sharp!

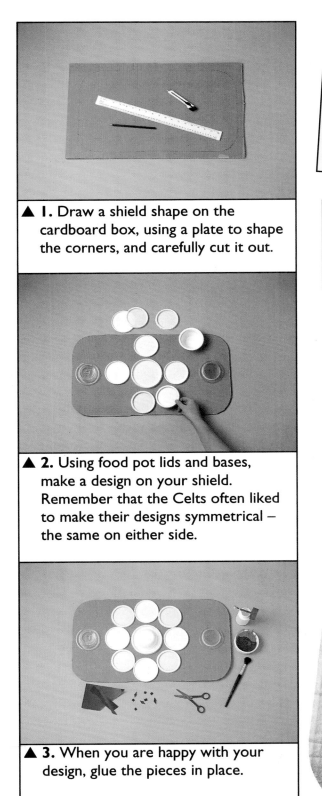

You will need: a large piece of thick cardboard ● a small plate ● a modelling knife ● empty plastic food pots and lids of various sizes ● a pencil ● a ruler ● PVA glue ● bronze-coloured paint ● scissors ● coloured paper or plastic "jewels"

▲ **1.** Draw a shield shape on the cardboard box, using a plate to shape the corners, and carefully cut it out.

▲ **2.** Using food pot lids and bases, make a design on your shield. Remember that the Celts often liked to make their designs symmetrical – the same on either side.

▲ **3.** When you are happy with your design, glue the pieces in place.

4. Paint the whole shield a bronze colour and add pieces of coloured paper and plastic "jewels" as decoration.

THE ROMANS IN BRITAIN

We know much more about the period when the Romans were in Britain than we do about earlier times. The Romans left written records of their activities, as well as many carved notices, called inscriptions, on monuments and buildings.

GOVERNING A NEW LAND

As a province of the Roman Empire, Britain had a Roman governor who was responsible for running the country. He appointed local governors for towns and areas. The Roman army was always active to remind people of the Romans' strength and to tackle any uprisings that took place. Many Roman soldiers settled in Britain when they retired.

Roman towns were built to a similar plan all over the empire, with straight streets, shops and houses, and a central market place called the forum. The Romans imported goods and food from all over the empire, helping Roman settlers to feel at home. Food plants such as carrots and peas were also introduced by the Romans. ▼

Tribes in the north of Scotland were never conquered by the Romans. In the second century AD the Emperor Hadrian had a wall built to stop them raiding further south. It was 120 kilometres (75 miles) long.

NEW WAYS OF LIVING

The Roman invaders brought many new ideas with them. Before the Romans came, there were no towns in Britain, only small villages. London, now the biggest city in Britain, was founded by the Romans.

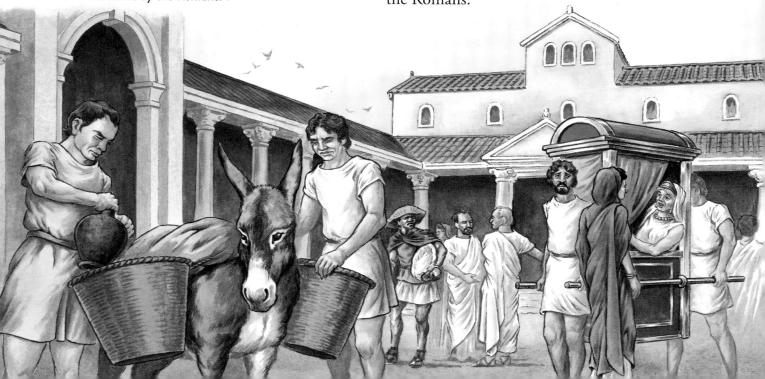

A WRITTEN LANGUAGE

The language of the Romans was Latin. They used it throughout their empire and every Roman soldier had to be able to read and write. Of course, Britons who lived and traded with the Romans had to learn Latin and many of them in the towns could read and write as well. For hundreds of years after the Romans left Britain, Latin was still used for official documents and in the Christian religion.

▲The Romans were skilled engineers. Their houses had plumbing and heating and they built roads and bridges throughout Britain. The Britons must have been astonished by the speed at which people and goods could be moved about the province.

This Roman mosaic floor from Fishbourne shows Cupid riding a dolphin, surrounded by sea beasts, sea horses and sea panthers.

MANY BELIEFS

During the time that the Romans were in Britain, the new religion of Christianity, based on the teachings of Jesus Christ, began to spread to all parts of the empire.

The religion of the ancient Britons was closely linked to the natural world and the importance of the seasons and the fertility of the soil. Priests called druids led ceremonies and made predictions. The religion of the Romans featured many gods, some of whom also represented the rhythms of nature.

As long as local religions did not threaten their rule, the Romans let them continue. At first the Romans tried to stop Christianity because Christians claimed that their first duty was to God, not earthly rulers, but later even the Roman emperors became Christians.

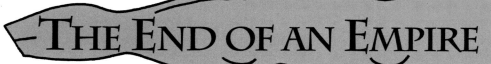
For nearly 400 years the Romans ruled a large part of the British Isles. Sometimes the Britons lived peacefully under Roman rule. But very often the Romans had to cope with uprisings by some of the British tribes or attacks from outside the borders of the empire.

A famous revolt happened only 16 years after the invasion. It was led by Boudica, queen of the Iceni tribe from East Anglia. Boudica's troops burnt down the town of Colchester and went on to attack and destroy London. The Roman governor, Suetonius, hurried back from Anglesey, where he was attacking other tribes, and crushed the British revolt.

A later Roman historian described Boudica as having red hair and "a large golden necklace". It may have been like this neck-ring, called a torque, found in Norfolk.

The problems that the Romans had in keeping order in Britain happened throughout the empire. As the empire grew, there were more people to control and more tribes outside the empire wanting to attack and steal from wealthy citizens. In AD 406 the Roman army finally left Britain to defend other parts of the empire. The end of the empire was very near and the Romans never returned.

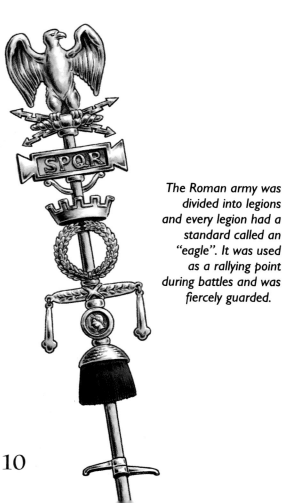

The Roman army was divided into legions and every legion had a standard called an "eagle". It was used as a rallying point during battles and was fiercely guarded.

MAKE A ROMAN STANDARD

You will need: a garden cane at least 1 metre long ●cardboard ●a pencil ●a pot-plant stake ●a paper plate ●paper ●a piece of red or purple cloth ●scissors ●sticky tape or glue ●gold paint

▲ **1.** Draw an eagle shape like this on a piece of card and cut it out carefully. It should be about twice as wide as the paper plate.

2. Draw round the paper plate on to card to make a crescent shape and cut it out.

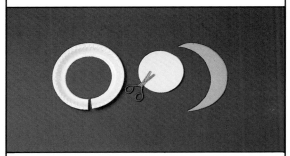

▲ **3.** Carefully cut the flat middle from the paper plate, making sure to cut the outer ring in only one place.

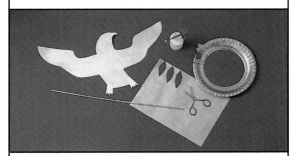

▲ **4.** Paint all the cut-out pieces and the pot-plant stake gold. Paint a piece of paper gold on both sides and cut out lots of leaf shapes. Stick them on to the ring from the paper plate to make a laurel wreath.

▲ **5.** Hang the red or purple cloth from the pot-plant stake. You can fray the bottom edge and paint it to make a gold fringe if you like. Use sticky tape to fix all the pieces one under the other on the cane.

11

While the Romans were in Britain, they defended their province from attacks by overseas tribes. But when the Roman army had gone, the British were at the mercy of invaders from northern Europe. Almost immediately, the people we describe as Anglo-Saxons began to attack the north-east coast of England.

WHO WERE THE ANGLO-SAXONS?

The people that we call Anglo-Saxons actually came from several different tribes: the Jutes from what is now Denmark, the Angles from northern Germany, and the Saxons and Frisians from parts of Germany and the Netherlands. Their pirate ships had raided the coast of Britain for years, but when the Romans left they were able to push further into the country with greater numbers of people.

The parts of Europe where the Anglo-Saxons lived were difficult to farm. They were wooded and marshy, with some areas being flooded by the sea. There was not enough good land to feed everyone, so the Anglo-Saxons hoped to find better farming land in Britain.

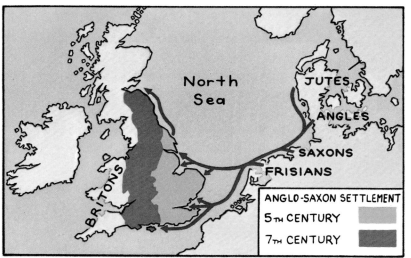

North Sea

JUTES

ANGLES

SAXONS

FRISIANS

BRITONS

ANGLO-SAXON SETTLEMENT

5TH CENTURY

7TH CENTURY

▲ As the Anglo-Saxons gradually occupied more and more of Britain, they pushed some of the Celtic Britons further westward. But other Britons lived peacefully alongside the newcomers. It is from the Angles that we get the words "England" and "English".

The Anglo-Saxons crossed the North Sea in big wooden rowing boats like this. The large oar was the rudder, used to steer the boat. The rowers pulled their oars against the slots on the side of the boat. This boat was found in a peat bog in Denmark.▼

THE ANGLO-SAXON STORY OF THE INVASION

Over 400 years after the Anglo-Saxons began to arrive, King Alfred ordered that a book should be written to tell the history of the Anglo-Saxons in Britain. This book has survived and is called The Anglo-Saxon Chronicle. The book says that after the Romans left, a British king called Vortigern gave some Saxons land in south-east England in return for helping him to fight the Picts, a Scottish tribe that the Romans never conquered. Angles and Jutes, as well as Saxons, came to Britain, led by two brothers, Hengist and Horsa. When they had helped the king, the Chronicle says, they turned against him and took over the kingdom.

▲This is a page from the Anglo-Saxon Chronicle. As the story was written down a long time after the events it describes, it is hard to tell whether it is true, but it is certainly possible that some Anglo-Saxons were invited to Britain.

HOW ANGLO-SAXONS LIVED

The Anglo-Saxons did not invade Britain all at once but gradually moved down the rivers and settled further and further west and south. In some places Roman systems of government may have continued for up to 200 years after the Romans left. Meanwhile some Celtic British groups were returning to the way of life they followed before the Romans came. So for some time there was a great mixture of people and ways of life in Britain.

The Anglo-Saxon farmers grew peas, beans, barley and wheat as well as hay for their animals to eat in the winter. They kept cattle, sheep, pigs, geese and hens. They also seem to have had pet cats and dogs.

Many pieces of Anglo-Saxon pottery have been found. Most of these were for everyday use, but some pots were used as urns in which to bury the ashes of dead people.

14

There was no tea or coffee in England in Anglo-Saxon times. Poor people drank a kind of beer, while rich people had wine or mead, made from honey and water.

Most Anglo-Saxon clothes were made from wool. They raised the sheep, spun, dyed and wove the wool themselves. The weaving looms had stones with holes in them to weight down the threads. They were used leaning against the wall of a house.

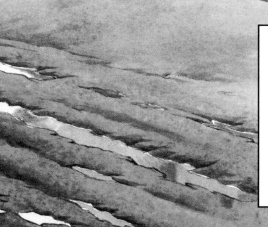

Clothes were held together with brooches. Women wore strings of coloured glass or stone beads. Some women wore strange key-like metal objects from their waists. Archaeologists are not sure what these were for. What do you think?

AN ANGLO-SAXON VILLAGE

Anglo-Saxon homes were usually built with a wooden framework. The walls were filled in with wooden planks or clay mixed with straw. Some of them seem to have had a space under the floor, perhaps for storage or to keep the floor dry.

A family home was quite small and probably had only one room. But the village also had a larger building, called a hall, where people could meet and eat together.

MAKE AN ANGLO-SAXON HALL

▲ At West Stow in Suffolk, archaeologists have discovered traces of an Anglo-Saxon village. After finding post holes in the ground, they were able to work out where the village buildings were and make some good guesses about how they were built. Then they used this knowledge to rebuild the village using the same tools and methods that the Anglo-Saxons used.

You will need: thick cardboard
• newspaper • scissors • PVA glue
• sticky tape • a large plastic container
• paints

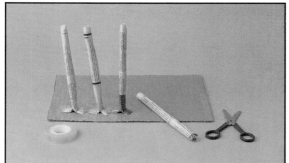

▲ **1.** Make a rectangular base about 35 cm long and 20 cm wide from a piece of strong cardboard. Then fold pieces of newspaper in halves and quarters and roll them up tightly. Use glue or sticky tape to make sure they don't unroll. Make two cuts at the end off each roll and glue or tape them evenly around the rectangle to make posts for your hall.

2. Trim the posts so that they are all the same level but shape the end ones as shown. Tape or glue more paper rolls across the posts as in the picture to make the framework for the roof and doors and windows.

▲ 3. Tear some more newspapers into small pieces and soak them in water overnight in the plastic container.

4. Mash up the paper a bit more with your fingers. Then squeeze out as much water as possible and mix in some PVA glue. Add enough so that the paper can be modelled into different shapes.

5. Use the paper mixture to fill in the walls of the hall, just as the Anglo-Saxons used clay and straw. Remember to leave some spaces for windows and doors.

Why not make lots of Anglo-Saxon buildings of different sizes and build a model village?

▲ 6. When the paper mixture has dried, make a cardboard roof for your hall and put it carefully on top of the walls. Make sure it has a hole in the middle for smoke from the fire to come out.

▲ 7. Paint your model and its base. You can add cardboard doors as well if you like.

Religious Life

Christianity had come to Britain in Roman times, but the Anglo-Saxons brought their own religion. They believed that different gods controlled different parts of their lives and what would happen to them after they died.

Woden was the chief of all the gods. Frig, his wife, made crops grow. Tiu was the war god, and Thunor the god of thunder and the sky.

Our only clues to how the Anglo-Saxons worshipped their gods come from the writings of Christian missionaries who said that they killed animals in their religious ceremonies. But the missionaries were trying to stamp out the Anglo-Saxon religion, so it is hard to know if this is true.

This Anglo-Saxon helmet and buckle are beautifully decorated. Often, Anglo-Saxon decorations contained images of the god Woden.

These objects were found in a grave at Sutton Hoo in Suffolk. An important man had been buried in a wooden boat that was 28 metres long. Many precious objects were buried with him. Although this was not a Christian burial, some objects with Bible names were found in the grave.▼

AN ANGLO-SAXON BURIAL

Many of the pieces of Anglo-Saxon jewellery, goods and clothing that have been found were discovered in graves. In pagan (not Christian) burials, it seems that people were buried with some of their precious possessions, perhaps because it was thought that they would need them in the next life.

THE RETURN OF CHRISTIANITY

By the time the Anglo-Saxons had been in Britain for about 200 years, Christianity was still practised in only a few western areas. Pope Gregory, the leader of the Christian religion in western Europe, sent a man called Augustine to England to convert the people to Christianity.

Christians believe that there is only one God and that he sent Jesus Christ to live on earth and show people how to act in this life and how they can live for ever with God after they die.

Augustine's first success was in converting Aethelbert, an Anglo-Saxon king living in Kent. The king allowed Augustine to use an old Roman church in Canterbury. Pope Gregory made Augustine Archbishop of Canterbury. This has been the title of the leader of the main Christian church in Britain ever since.

MONASTERIES

Because the Anglo-Saxons did not invade Ireland, the people there were still Christians since Roman times. About 30 years before Augustine came to England, an Irish monk called Columba sailed to Iona, a small island off the western coast of Scotland, and built a monastery.

Monks are men who have decided to live together and make worshipping God the most important part of their lives. The place where they live is called a monastery. Women who do the same thing are called nuns. They live in a nunnery or convent.

Christianity spread across northern England and another famous monastery was built on the island of Lindisfarne, just off the coast of Northumbria.

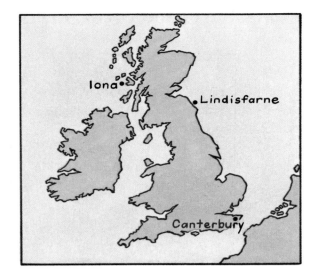

▲ *Lindisfarne's isolated position off the coast, later made it easy for raider's from the sea to attack.*

Monasteries were important centres of learning for hundreds of years. The monks studied the Bible, the book that describes the life of Jesus Christ and the history of the people he lived among, and many other subjects. They wrote books by hand and often decorated them with beautiful coloured drawings.

◄ *This is a page from the Lindisfarne Gospels. The Gospels are the part of the Bible that describes the life of Jesus. The book was copied out by hand and has many beautiful decorations. It is written in the Latin language on vellum, which is made from calf's skin.*

MAKE AN ILLUMINATED MANUSCRIPT

▲ **1.** Dip the sponge in the cold tea and dab it across the paper to make it look old. You could roughen or tear the edges a little bit too. Make the places where you think fingers would touch the page to turn it over a little darker still.

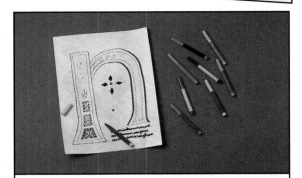

▲ **3.** Colour your design using felt-tip pens. To complete it, highlight some parts with the gold felt-tip pen.

▲ **2.** Design your page carefully in pencil. Make one big letter with decorations or little pictures to take up most of the page, then add some smaller writing at the end. You could copy the manuscripts on pages 13 or 20 or make up your own design using your name.

21

THE RULERS OF BRITAIN

When the Anglo-Saxons first came to Britain, they lived in small family groups. As they took control of more of England, they became organised into larger groups with a local chief or king. The names given to the areas under each king remain today in some of our county names. If Essex means "the kingdom of the East Saxons", what do you think Wessex and Sussex might mean?

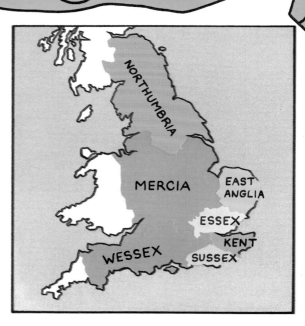

As well as the main kingdoms shown on the map, there were probably many independent kings ruling small areas.

Each person had a different place and a different value in the kingdom. The Anglo-Saxons actually developed a system called "wergild" to set a value on people. This meant that each person was worth an amount of money.

The king was worth a lot of money, while a slave was worth very little. Everyone else came somewhere in between. If a person was killed, the killer had to pay the victim's family the amount he or she was worth.

As some of the kingdoms became more powerful, they tried to take over neighbouring areas. The first man to call himself "King of the English" was Offa, king of Mercia. His power and influence reached into the other kingdoms south of the River Humber.

▲*This great bank of earth with a ditch running beside it was built on the orders of King Offa. It is 238 kilometres long, stretching the length of Wales and separating it from Mercia. We don't know for certain why Offa's Dyke was built, but it shows that he was powerful.*

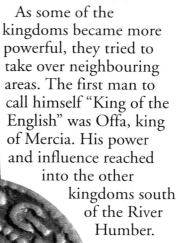

◄ *Offa had coins made with his name stamped on them.*

22

Offa ruled from 757 to 796, but by the time of his death, a new danger was threatening the peace of Britain. Once again, raiders from northern Europe were attacking. In 793 Vikings attacked the monastery at Lindisfarne and destroyed it.

The Vikings were excellent seamen and fierce fighters who came from Denmark, Norway and Sweden. For over 200 years they raided the coasts of Europe, but as traders they travelled even further – to Russia and central Asia. Some people think that they reached America as well, 600 years before Christopher Columbus.

Many of the Vikings who attacked Britain came from Denmark and were known as Danes, Northmen or Norsemen.

The Anglo-Saxons were very afraid of the Viking raiders. A common prayer was, "From the fury of the Northmen, good Lord deliver us."

At first the Vikings were mainly interested in raiding – taking what valuables they could find and disappearing again. But as time went on, the Vikings wanted more from Britain. Like the Anglo-Saxons before them, they did not have enough farming land at home to feed everyone and needed to find new lands. In 860 a large army of Vikings arrived from Denmark. The Anglo-Saxons called these Danes the "Great Army".

The Great Army attacked East Anglia and Northumbria and killed their kings. Then they moved into Mercia. Finally, only Wessex was not controlled by the new invaders.

▲*After their defeat in 878, the Danes agreed to settle in the area shown in orange.*

ALFRED "THE GREAT"

When a man called Alfred became King of Wessex, the Danes had already been attacking for some time. The leader of the Great Army, Guthrun, attacked Alfred at Chippenham during the Christmas celebrations, forcing the king to escape and hide at Athelney, in the marshes of Somerset. But from there Alfred organised his forces and defeated the Danes at Edington in 878.

DANELAW

The Danes agreed to leave Wessex, part of Mercia and south-east England alone and to settle in Northumbria, East Anglia and the rest of Mercia. This area was known as Danelaw. Guthrun became a Christian.

◀ *After defeating the Danes, Alfred built fortified towns, called "burhs", where people could be safe if the Danes attacked again. This is where our word "borough" comes from. Like Roman towns hundreds of years before, Alfred's burhs had a rectangular shape and straight streets. This is a photograph of Wareham, Dorset, where the burh's street plan can still be seen.*

This jewel was found in 1693, near Athelney. Words around the jewel say, "Aelfred mec heht gewyrcan" meaning "Alfred had me made". It shows what a wealthy and powerful man Alfred was.

THE IMPORTANCE OF LEARNING

Although he himself only learnt to read and write when he was grown up, Alfred was concerned about the Anglo-Saxon language and education.

He had several important Latin books translated into Anglo-Saxon, which is an early form of our modern English language. The Anglo-Saxon Chronicle was begun by him. Alfred's actions helped to create the feeling of a country with a history – an idea of "Englishness".

While Alfred made his position safe in the south, more and more Vikings settled in northern England, trading with other parts of Europe. Wealthy towns grew up at places such as York and Nottingham.

ENGLAND AFTER ALFRED

It was Alfred's grandson, Athelstan, who, 50 years after Alfred fled to Athelney, marched his armies north and made the Viking and Welsh kings swear loyalty to him. For the first time, one man really was King of England, with most of Wales and Scotland also under his rule. But Athelstan and the kings who came after him still had battles to fight.

Nearly 40 years after Athelstan's death, the Vikings once again began to attack Britain. King Ethelred agreed to pay money to the Danes if they would go home! This was called "Danegeld" and for a while it worked. But in 1013 King Swein of Denmark attacked and seized the throne, beginning nearly 30 years of Danish rule.

Saxons
924 – 39 Athelstan
939 – 46 Edmund
946 – 55 Edred
955 – 59 Edwy
959 – 75 Edgar
975 – 78 Edward (the Martyr)
978 – 1013 Ethelred (the Unready)

Danes
1013 – 14 Swein
1014 – 35 Cnut
1035 – 40 Harold I
1040 – 42 Harthacnut

Saxons
1042 – 66 Edward the Confessor
1066 Harold II

Normans
William I (the Conqueror)

Swein's son, Cnut, married Emma, the widow of Ethelred. She was a Norman princess from Normandy in northern France. When Edward the Confessor died without any children in 1066, he promised the throne to William, the Duke of Normandy, but the English decided to crown Harold, the Earl of Wessex instead.

As soon as Harold was crowned, he faced trouble. The Norwegians invaded northern England in September and Harold marched north to defeat them. In the meantime, William landed in Sussex to claim the throne. Harold's exhausted army met the Normans at Hastings and Harold was killed.

The Bayeux tapestry, which shows the story of William's claim to the English throne, was embroidered by Anglo-Saxon women in France. This part shows the death of King Harold.

William's coronation on Christmas Day, 1066, marked the end of Anglo-Saxon rule in England but William's position was not yet secure. Accepting the crown of the Anglo-Saxon kings was one of his first acts to take control of the kingdom.

◀ *This engraving shows William being crowned King of England at Westminster Abbey.*

MAKE WILLIAM'S CROWN

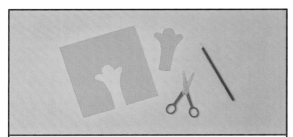

You will need: thin card • a ruler • a pencil • scissors • gold paint • paper clips

▲ **1.** Draw a shape on to thin card and cut it out carefully. Make it about 12 cm high.

▲ **2.** Take a piece of card about 50 cm long and draw a line right along it 6 cm from the edge. Make a mark at 5 cm along the line, at 15 cm, 25 cm, 35 cm and 45 cm.

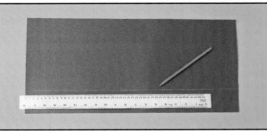

▲ **3.** At each mark draw round your card shape above the line.

4. Carefully cut out the crown and paint it gold. Fix the two ends together with paper clips or sticky tape, overlapping the ends to give a good fit.

THE INVADERS LEGACY

All the invaders of Britain from the Romans to the Normans have left traces of their lives that we can still see today.

PLACE NAMES

The names of our towns and villages are clues to who lived there in the past. The Romans, the Anglo-Saxons and the Vikings used their own languages to name places. Sometimes the spelling of these has changed over the years. Look at the lists below. Then find a map of your area and see if you can tell which people named the towns and villages nearby. Books about place names in your local library will give you even more information about their meaning.

Roman place names

camp	=	plain
caster	=	fort
eccles	=	church
port	=	harbour
wic	=	town

THE ENGLISH LANGUAGE

Some of our names for the days of the week also come from Britain's invaders. Sunday and Monday are named after the sun and moon, while Saturday takes its name from the Roman god, Saturn. Look at pages 18 and 19 and see if you can work out where the names of the other days of the week come from.

Answers The Anglo-Saxon words mean: cold, penny, kiss, ground, abbot, long, English. Look on page 24 for a clue to "gewyrcan" and remember that in order to make something, you have to "work."

Anglo-Saxon place names

burg, borough	=	fortified place
den, dene	=	valley
ea, ey	=	river
feld, field	=	field
ford	=	shallow river crossing
ham	=	settlement home
head	=	hill
holt	=	dense wood
ing	=	people
lea, leigh, ley	=	clearing
mere	=	lake
sted, stead	=	place
stoke, stow	=	meeting place
ton, tun	=	farm or village
wald	=	wood
wic, wick, wich	=	farm
worth	=	hedged land

Viking place names

by	=	village
thorpe	=	small village

Many other common English words come from Anglo-Saxon. Below are a few of them:

cald, penig, cyssan, grund, abbod, lang, Englisc, gewyrcan

Can you guess what they mean? Look at the box on the left if you get stuck.

DID YOU KNOW?

Until about 9,000 years ago, Britain was joined to the rest of Europe. People could simply walk across. But gradually the sea rose and Britain became an island. The only way to reach it was by boat.

When the Emperor Claudius came to Colchester to accept the surrender of some British leaders, he even brought a few elephants along to impress the Britons with his power! Of course, they had never seen such creatures before.

One way of writing Anglo-Saxon words was to use "runes". You can see which letters the runes stood for below. The Anglo-Saxons seem to have thought that the runes themselves were magic. They wrote the alphabet on rings as a charm against illness and danger.

In a way the Vikings really did succeed in conquering Britain. The Normans who invaded in 1066 were descended from "Norsemen" who had settled in northern France 200 years earlier.

The legend of King Arthur and his knights of the round table is set in the period when Anglo-Saxon raiders were attacking British tribes. All the old writings about Arthur date from hundreds of years later, so it is very hard to tell whether a British king called Arthur really existed.

f	u	th	o	r	k	g	w	h	n	i	j	h	p

x	s	t	b	e	m	l	ng	d	o	e	a	ae	y	ea

29

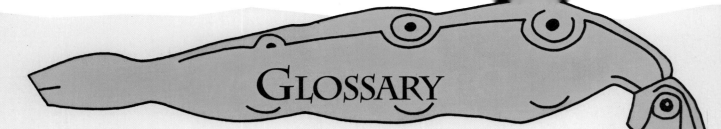

GLOSSARY

archaeologist – someone who studies objects from past times, often those that are buried in the ground.

burh – a fortified town that King Alfred ordered to be built.

Danegeld – money paid by Anglo-Saxon kings to Danish leaders to try to stop them from invading Britain.

daub – mud or clay used to fill the gaps in walls made of wattle.

earthwork – a structure made mainly of earth and stones, often as a place of safety.

empire – a large area of land, often made up of different countries, ruled over by one person, an emperor or empress.

forum – the main square and market place of a Roman town.

inscription – written words, especially those on a building, gravestone or coin.

invader – a person who moves into a new area without the permission of people already living there.

javelin – a kind of spear that could be thrown at the enemy.

legion – a body of between 3,000 and 6,000 men in the Roman army.

missionary – a person who tries to convert others to a particular religious faith.

monastery – a place where monks live – Christians who live together to devote their lives to God.

monument – a building or statue put up to remind people of a person or event.

rudder – a piece of wood under a boat that can be turned to change the boat's direction.

settler – a person who makes his or her home in a new place.

torque – a necklace of twisted metal made by the ancient Britons.

vellum – calf's skin made smooth so that it could be written on.

wattle – twigs woven together to make walls.

wergild – an Anglo-Saxon system of setting a value of money on each person. If the person was killed, the killer could pay that money to the family of the victim and avoid further punishment.

RESOURCES

Many museums have objects from Celtic, Roman, Anglo-Saxon, Viking or Norman times. Small local museums often have things on display that have been found very near where you live. The British Museum in London has very important finds from these periods.

PLACES TO VISIT

West Stow village
West Stow
near Bury St Edmunds
Suffolk IP28 6HG
Tel: (0284) 728718

Opening Times: 1000 – 1700 every day, all year.

This is an Anglo-Saxon village that has been reconstructed. There are also demonstrations of Anglo-Saxon crafts and events where people dress up in Anglo-Saxon costume and recreate village life.

Jorvik Viking Centre
Coppergate
York YO1 1NT
Tel: (0904) 643211

Opening Times: 1st April until 1st October: 0900 – 1900. From 1st November until 31st March: 0900 – 1730.

Jorvik is the Viking name for York. Archaeologists have reconstructed scenes from everyday life and visitors can travel by "time-car" through the sights, sounds and smells of Viking York.

The British Museum
Great Russell Street
London
WC1B 3DG
Tel: 071 636 1555 – 8

Opening Times: 1000 – 1700 Monday to Saturday; 1430 – 1800 Sunday. Closed 24th – 27th December, New Year's Day, May Bank Holiday and Good Friday.

The Museum has beautiful objects from all the periods in this book. The Anglo-Saxon Chronicle and most of the "treasures" from Roman and Anglo-Saxon times that have been found are on display there.

BOOKS TO READ

There are many books on this period of British history. You should find some in your local or school library. A few to look out for are:

The Ancient Britons by Pamela Odijk (Macmillan, 1989)

What Do We Know About the Celts? by Hazel Mary Martell (Simon & Schuster Young Books, 1993)

Romans by Nicola Baxter (Franklin Watts, 1992)

Roman Invaders and Settlers by Barry Marsden (Wayland, 1992)

The Anglo-Saxons by Rowena Loverance (BBC Educational Publishing, 1992)

Saxon Invaders and Settlers by Tony D. Triggs (Wayland, 1992)

The Anglo-Saxon Resource Book by James Mason (Longman, 1991)

Vikings by Rachel Wright (Franklin Watts, 1992)

INDEX

Additional Photographs:

Ancient Art & Architecture Collection 9, 10, 18, 20, 22, 26; British Library 13; ET Archive 6, 18, 24; Michael Halford 18, 19; Mansell Collection 27; Zefa 5, 8